A HOLE IN THE HEAD

For Isla, Woody and Freya ~ S.E.

For Nana Jane, made of
strong stuff! ~ S.C.

HODDER CHILDREN'S BOOKS
First published in Great Britain in 2025 by
Hodder and Stoughton

Text copyright © Dr Suzie Edge, 2025
Illustrations copyright © Sam Caldwell, 2025

PB ISBN 978-1-444-97533-8
E-book ISBN 978-1-444-97534-5

1 3 5 7 9 10 8 6 4 2

Printed in China

FSC
www.fsc.org
MIX
Paper | Supporting
responsible forestry
FSC® C104740

Hodder Children's Books
An imprint of Hachette Children's Group
Part of Hodder and Stoughton Limited
Carmelite House, 50 Victoria Embankment, London, EC4Y 0DZ

An Hachette UK Company
www.hachette.co.uk
www.hachettechildrens.co.uk

The authorised representative in the EEA is Hachette Ireland,
8 Castlecourt Centre, Dublin 15, D15 XTP3, Ireland (email: info@hbgi.ie)

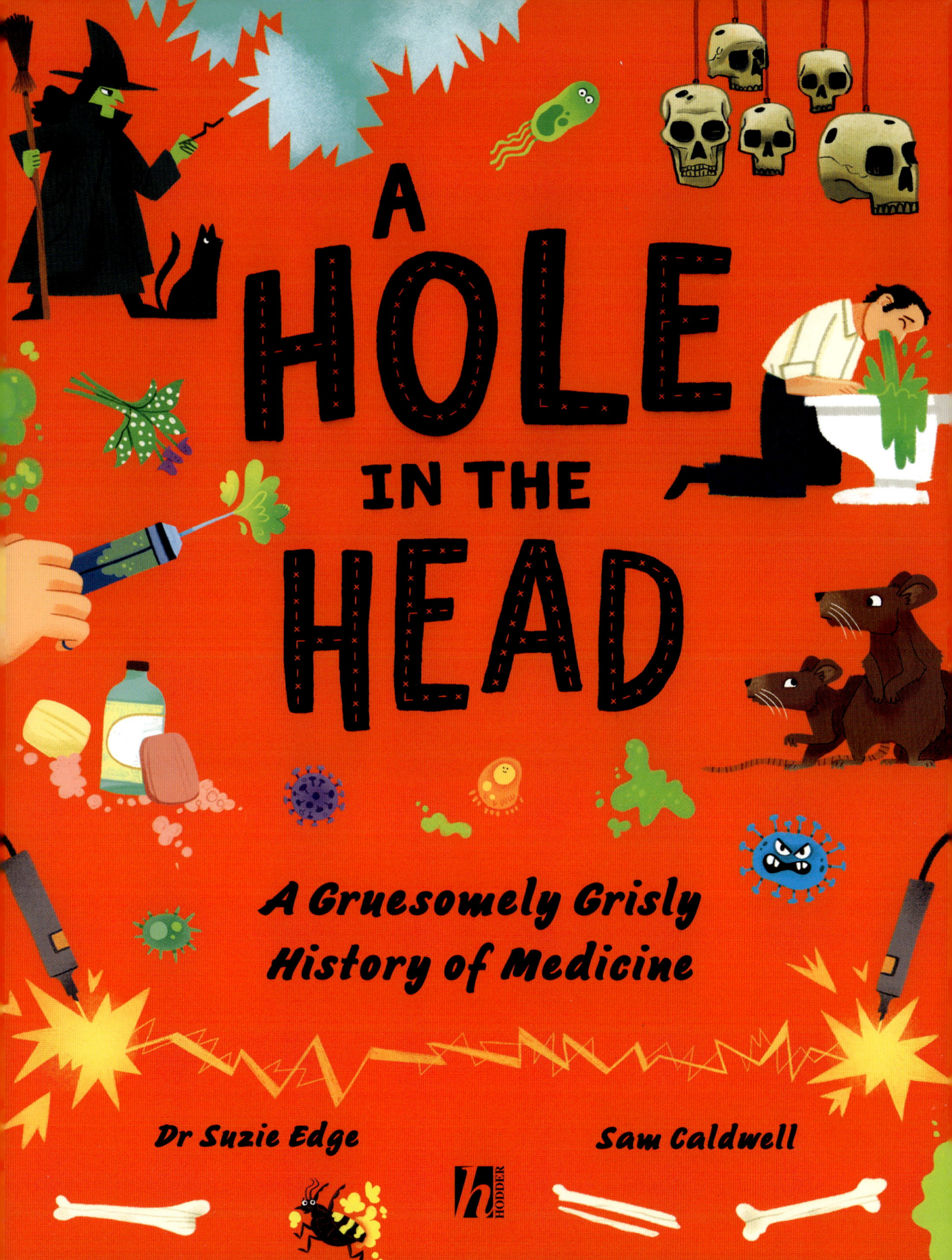

A HOLE IN THE HEAD

A Gruesomely Grisly
History of Medicine

Dr Suzie Edge

Sam Caldwell

HODDER

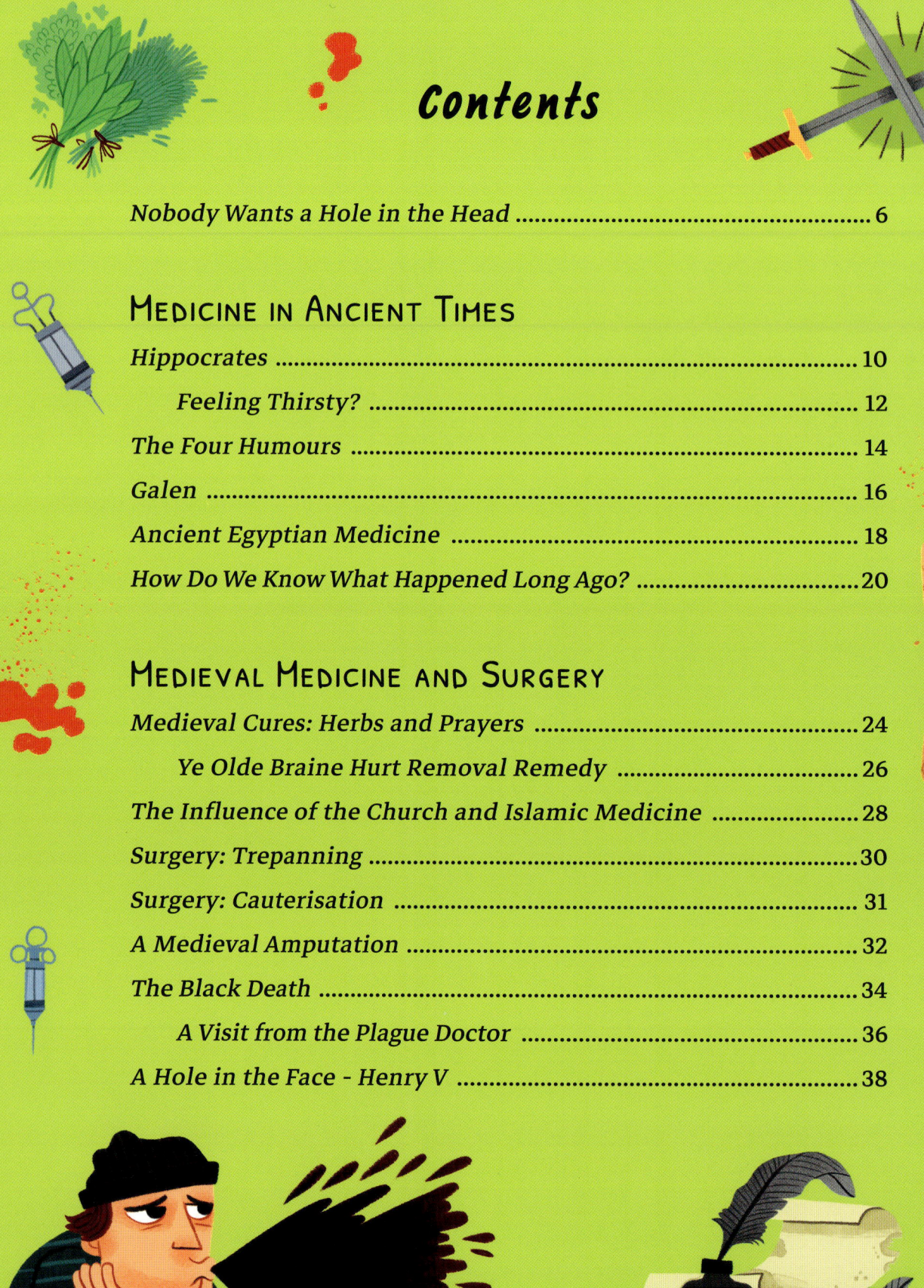

Contents

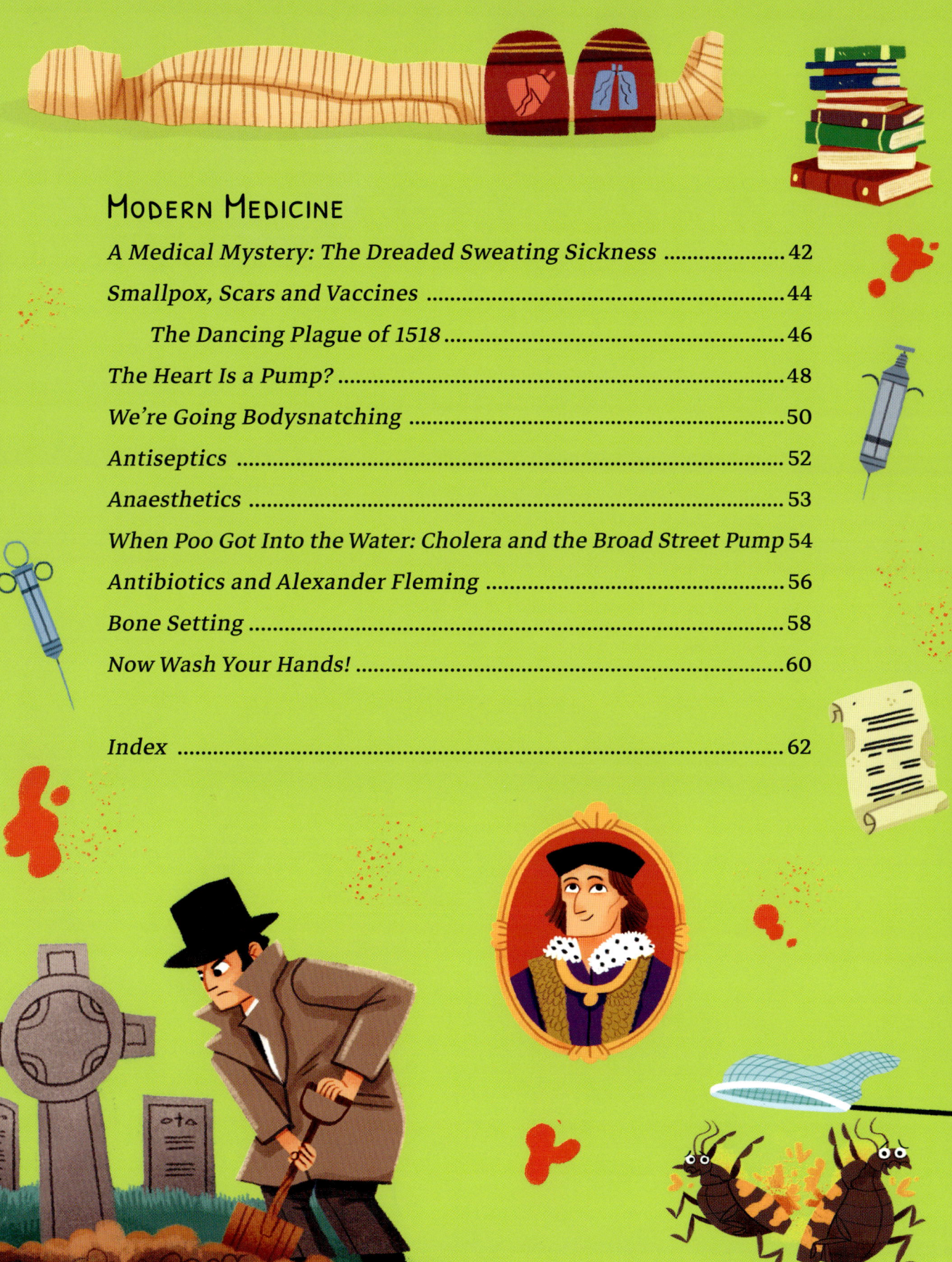

MODERN MEDICINE

Nobody Wants
A HOLE IN THE HEAD

Being sick is just horrible, so it's a good job there are people who want to help. Over the centuries, we humans have tried all sorts of lotions and potions, surgeries and prayers to cure sick people. Some were even successful! A lot haven't worked one bit.

From 5,000 years ago in ancient Mesopotamia to your local hospital just yesterday, we can trace how human beings have dealt with disease. In this book, we're going to take a trip through the ancient world, medieval times and the modern era to see for ourselves how coughs and sneezes, tummy bugs and broken limbs have all been treated. Watch out, or you might get a hole in the head!

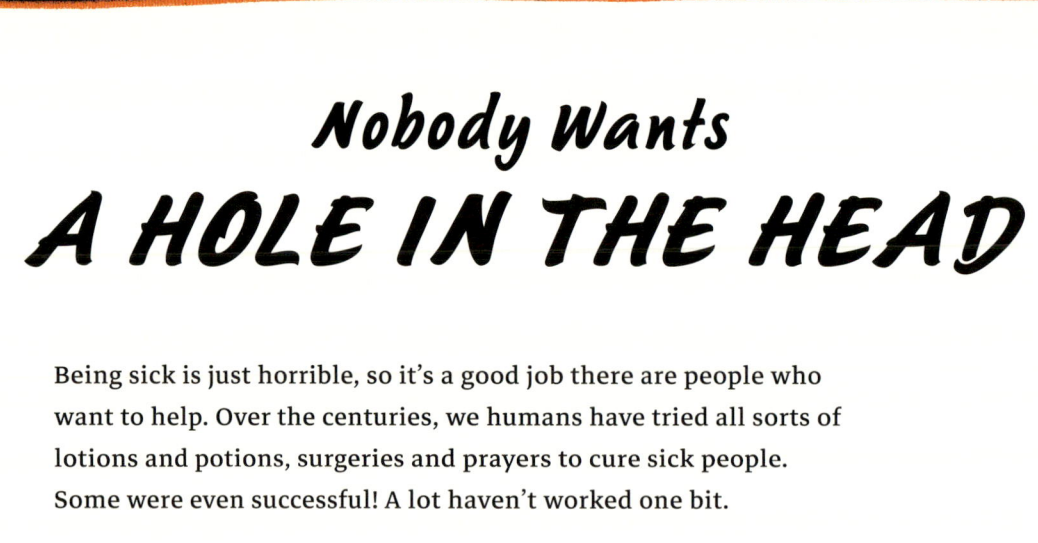

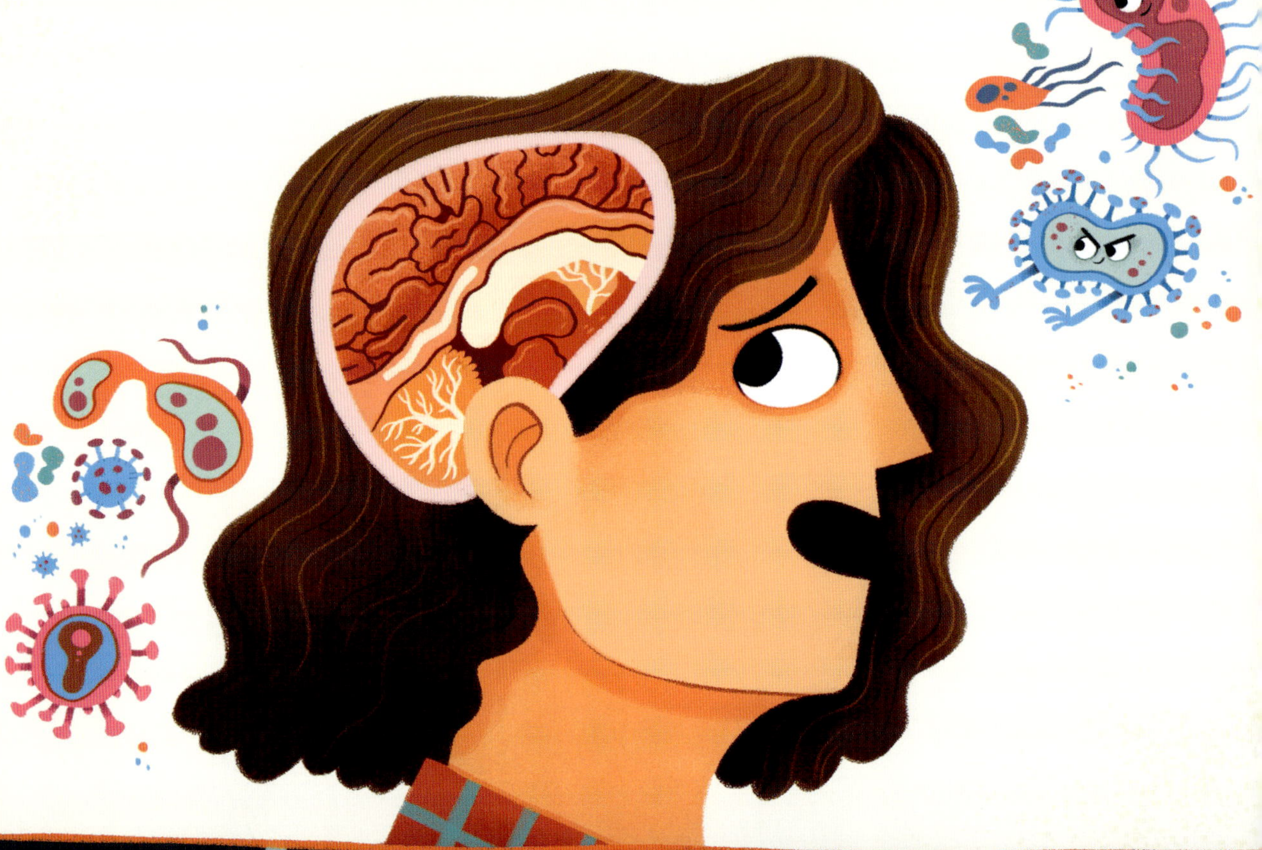

In ancient times, people understood the idea that preventing illnesses was better than having to try and cure them. They left us clay tablets and scrolls, and that's how we know what they did.

Medieval doctors learned a lot about the body and surgery during times of war, which, sadly, is where new medical understanding often comes from. A lot of people can be hurt very quickly during fights, and armies of soldiers living and moving about together can spread all kinds of diseases.

In the modern era, there have been so many medical discoveries for the good. We started to understand germs and how to prevent and treat them. We learned more about how the human body works. (Even if we sometimes had to steal dead bodies from graveyards to do it!) We got much better at surgery and created remarkable vaccines. Now we have clean and much safer medicines and operations, thanks to all the wonderful experiments and medical firsts.

But the human body can be smelly and sticky, so hold on to your noses, and let's dive in.

MEDICINE IN ANCIENT TIMES

When we talk about ancient societies, we think of the places where they lived, like ancient Mesopotamia and ancient Greece, Egypt and Rome.

In these places, thousands of years ago, philosophers (thinkers) and physicians (doctors) would study the human body and write down how they would treat illnesses. Some of their ideas are very funny to us today. In the future, people might look at our treatments and think we were funny too!

For many hundreds of years, whenever anyone was sick, we looked to the ancient civilisations and what they had to say about disease and medicines. The ancient scrolls were copied and passed around, taken around the world on voyages and translated into different languages.

In ancient Greece, a doctor called Hippocrates wrote about how to look after sick people. However, he did some strange things too, like tasting earwax and all things gooey! Ew.

Later, in ancient Rome, Galen read Hippocrates' work and added his own ideas to it. Today we still use some of the treatments and surgery techniques that the ancients wrote about. Thanks, Ancients! We're lucky that the texts have lasted as long as they have over all those years.

Want to know what Hippocrates did with pee? Let's go back a few thousand years and see how the ancients dealt with the poorly.

PEE

Hippocrates

BORN: Around 460 BCE – nearly 2,500 years ago! – on the Greek island of Kos.

DIED: 375 BCE

NICKNAME: The Father of Medicine. Thanks, Dad!

LOVED: The four humours.

WROTE: The *Hippocratic Corpus*, a big collection of books that tells us what he studied and taught others.

LEGACY: The Hippocratic Oath – a promise made by doctors that they will try their best to help people and that they won't knowingly do any harm.

Isn't it brilliant that we know who Hippocrates was and what he did to help people so long ago? He understood the importance of knowing how the human body works in the first place, and that's why he studied **anatomy** (all the parts of the body and how they fit together). Hippocrates also said the body was made up of the four humours. They're gross and sticky, and there's more where they came from on page 14.

Sickness was a problem to be solved, like a giant human-sized puzzle. Hippocrates believed that careful observation, looking closely at the diseases and trying different treatments to see if they worked was the key to solving the medical puzzles. Are you good at puzzles? If so, you might make a great doctor! You may even be asked to say the **Hippocratic oath** one day, which is a code of principles, such as not causing harm and giving only beneficial treatments, for medical teachers and their students.

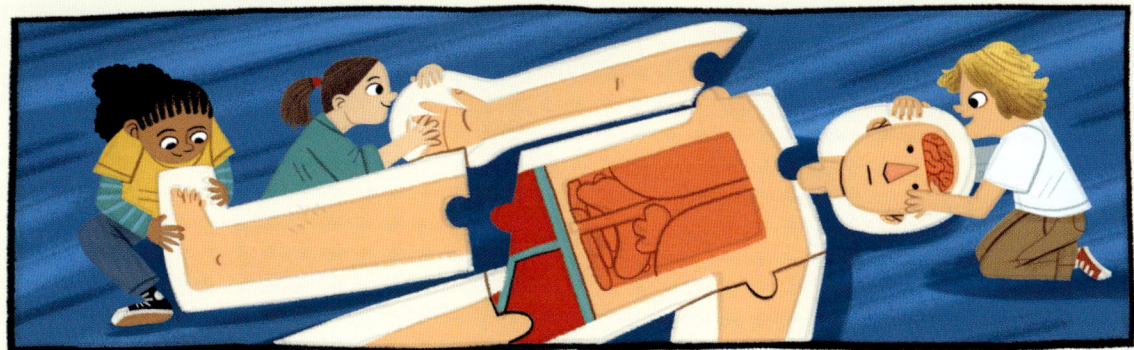

But Hippocrates had some unconventional and outright DISGUSTING ways of solving puzzles. It involves sniffing and tasting . . . well, you can guess what he sniffed and tasted! Turn the page if you're ready to be grossed out . . .

HIPPOCRATES WAS KNOWN TO **TASTE** WEE (AFTER SNIFFING IT!) TO SEE HOW SICK HIS PATIENTS WERE.

You can tell a lot about somebody's health from their urine – no magnifying glass needed!

Hold it in for a moment! I have this wee to inspect first.

PEE GUIDE

DARK OR BROWN = NOT DRINKING ENOUGH

LIGHT OR STRAW COLOURED = MIGHT BE DRINKING TOO MUCH

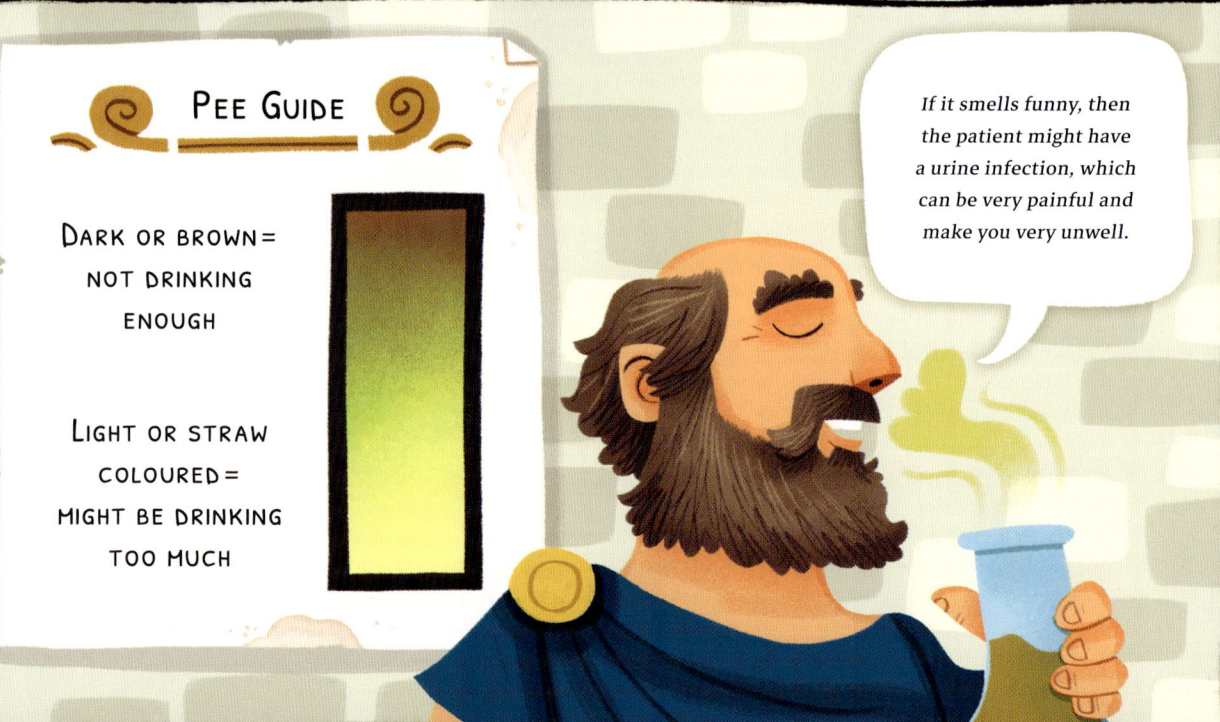

If it smells funny, then the patient might have a urine infection, which can be very painful and make you very unwell.

For many hundreds of years, Hippocrates had people believing that the body was made up of four liquids called the four humours. They weren't that funny, though.

They were called **blood**, **phlegm**, **black bile** and **yellow bile**. It was thought that having more of any of the humours said something about someone's personality.

For example, someone with lots of blood could be active and chatty!

Or someone who is always down in the dumps is melancholic, meaning full of black bile.

Diseases made the humours go all funny and out of balance. The way to treat disease, then, was to balance the humours back up. That would mean taking liquids away. But how was that done?

Bleeding, or **bloodletting**, was when doctors would cut open a vein and let some blood drain out. Did you know that it is thought George Washington, the first President of the United States of America, died because doctors took too much blood off him when he was sick? He needed his blood to carry oxygen and nutrients about his body!

UMMM, I THINK I MIGHT NEED TO KEEP SOME OF THAT!

Another way to balance the humours was to make somebody be **sick**. They were given nasty medicines to drink that would make them bring up their breakfast. Or there was always the other end! People could be given medicines that would make them poo and poo and POO until lots of liquid came out too. YUCK!

AAAAARGH, IT'S COMING OUT BOTH ENDS!

Then there was **blistering**. Have you ever had a blister? Maybe when new shoes have rubbed your skin? Blisters are full of liquid, and if you pop them (POP!) the liquid comes out. That was another way of balancing the fluids. Sick people weren't given new shoes, though, so how were they blistered? Sometimes skin would be burned with a blisteringly hot iron (OUCH!), but there was another way too.

OUCH!

HELP!

There's a special beetle called a blister beetle. They are small, but they can be spotted easily because some have bright red and yellow colouring. But that's a warning: DON'T TOUCH ME OR I WILL MAKE YOUR SKIN BLISTER! Someone very clever – but a bit mean to beetles – realised if you crush up the beetles you can put the paste on skin and make it blister, bringing lots of fluid out that you can wash away. OUCH AGAIN!

Through the ages, doctors have used many ways to balance the bodily humours to try and help the sick – but let's be glad today's doctors don't use blistering beetle paste!

Galen

BORN: 192 CE – nearly 2,000 years ago.

NAME: Claudius Galenus (but known as Galen).

TRAINED AS A DOCTOR: Greece.

PRACTISED AS A DOCTOR: During the time of the Roman Empire.

NOTABLE PATIENTS: Emperors Marcus Aurelius, Lucius Verus, Commodus and Septimius Severus.

OFTEN WOULD: Dissect dead animals and humans to learn what they were made of.

WROTE: *On the Natural Faculties and Method of Medicine*, a bit like a WHAT and HOW of looking after the sick.

Galen liked to learn everything there was to know about the human body:

Anatomy: what the body parts are and what they are made of.

Physiology: how the body parts all work together.

Pathology: when the body goes wrong with disease.

Pharmacology: how medicines work.

He believed in the four humours and balancing them out too, but he took it further. He liked the ideas of balancing **opposites**, like hot against cold or dry against wet. If he had a patient who was hot and dry, he would treat them with cucumber, because it was cold and wet!

Galen also believed that simply making his patients think he knew what he was doing was enough to cure their illnesses. It would be nice for doctors if that worked!

For a long time, people turned to Galen for answers, but after a while, people started to question him. Were his writings correct? Were these treatments really working? In the fourteenth century, when the Black Death came to Europe, people wondered: "What does Galen say we should do about this deadly plague?" Doctors looked to the works of Galen to see what he had to say, but they found he made no mention of plague at all. "Well, what does he even know about medicine then?" they asked.

He hadn't written about plague because he hadn't seen it for himself, so that would be impossible. Still, from then on, people questioned Galen's work. Poor Galen!

Ancient Egyptian Medicine

What would an ancient Egyptian do if somebody hurt themselves? They believed that diseases like tummy aches and sore knees were sent by the Gods and demons.

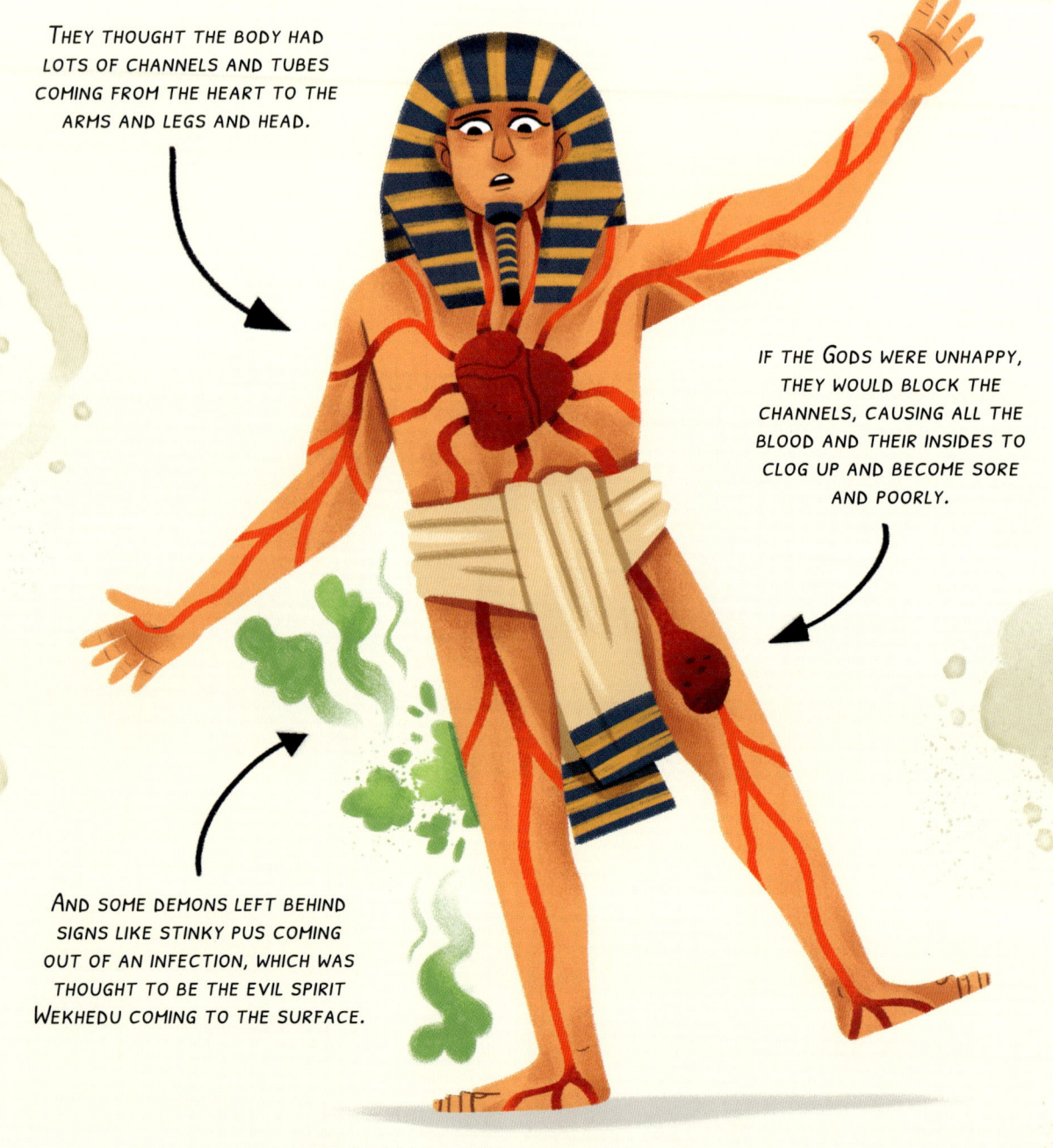

THEY THOUGHT THE BODY HAD LOTS OF CHANNELS AND TUBES COMING FROM THE HEART TO THE ARMS AND LEGS AND HEAD.

IF THE GODS WERE UNHAPPY, THEY WOULD BLOCK THE CHANNELS, CAUSING ALL THE BLOOD AND THEIR INSIDES TO CLOG UP AND BECOME SORE AND POORLY.

AND SOME DEMONS LEFT BEHIND SIGNS LIKE STINKY PUS COMING OUT OF AN INFECTION, WHICH WAS THOUGHT TO BE THE EVIL SPIRIT WEKHEDU COMING TO THE SURFACE.

So, disease was caused by angry gods and demons, but the Egyptians knew they could help themselves.

They had medical textbooks to look up the answers, just like we do! They had what is now known as the *Edwin Smith Papyrus*, the oldest known book on how to deal with trauma (that's when we get hurt). It was a collection of treatments that taught:

How to pull teeth out with pliers.

How to saw through bones to cut off broken legs and arms.

How to use scalpels (which are very sharp small knives).

Have you ever had stitches on a cut? About 2,500 years ago in ancient Egypt, they did the same thing, though maybe not in a bright and clean hospital, like today.

The ancient Egyptians also prayed. The god Bes was believed to protect women who were going to have a baby, and Heka was a goddess of magic and medicine. Unlucky enough to be bitten by a scorpion? Then pray to Serket to help immediately!

It may be surprising, but in ancient Egypt it wasn't just men who were the doctors. Peseshet was a female physician who was known as the 'Lady Overseer of Female Physicians', so she was pretty important and likely led a whole team of women.

And how did the ancient Egyptians know so much about how the body was made? **Mummification**! When someone died, the Egyptians would cut the body up and preserve it. Making a mummy could take up to 70 days and involved removing the organs. That's a great way to discover the ins and outs of the human body!

How Do We Know What Happened Long Ago?

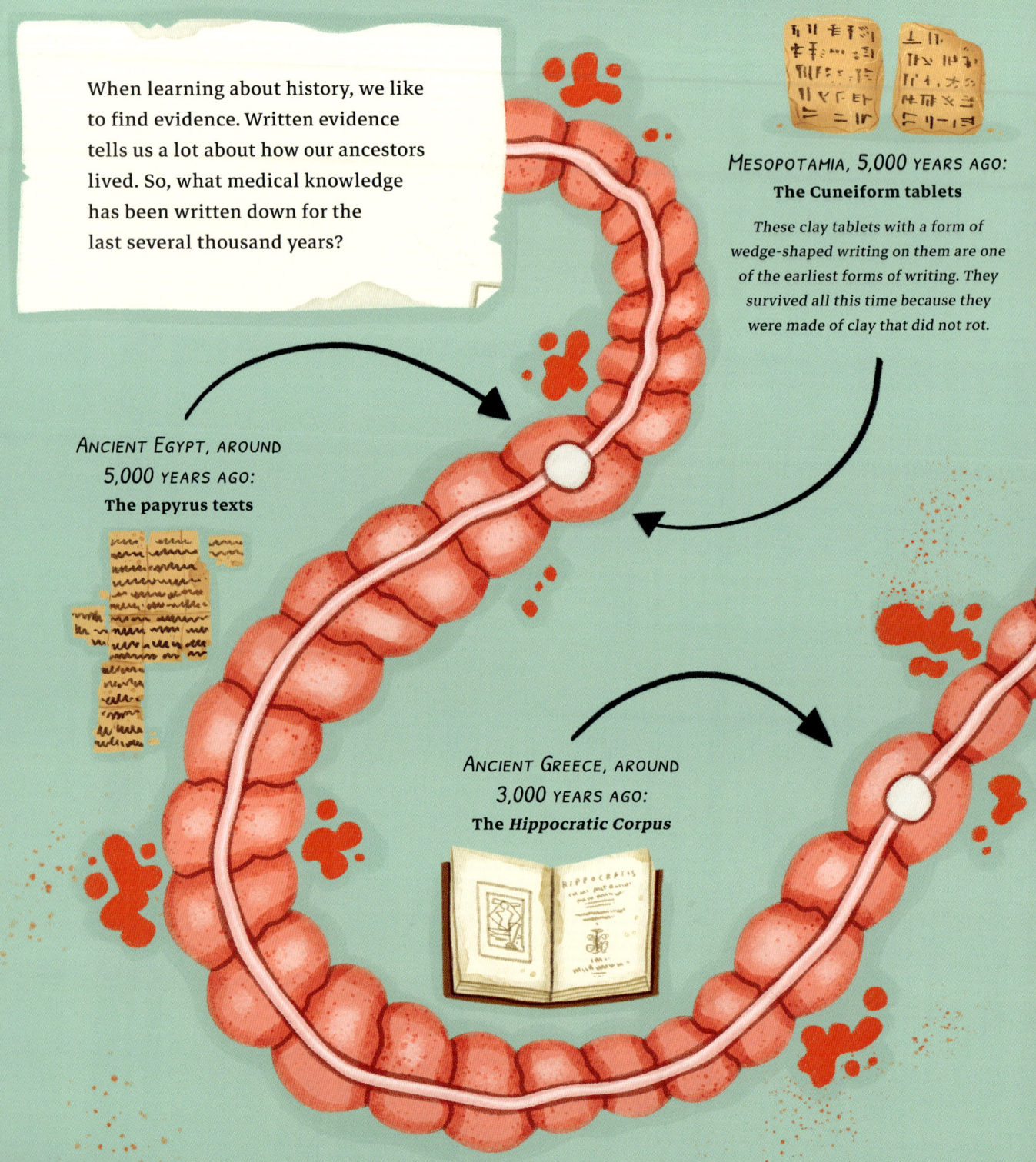

When learning about history, we like to find evidence. Written evidence tells us a lot about how our ancestors lived. So, what medical knowledge has been written down for the last several thousand years?

MESOPOTAMIA, 5,000 YEARS AGO:
The Cuneiform tablets

These clay tablets with a form of wedge-shaped writing on them are one of the earliest forms of writing. They survived all this time because they were made of clay that did not rot.

ANCIENT EGYPT, AROUND 5,000 YEARS AGO:
The papyrus texts

ANCIENT GREECE, AROUND 3,000 YEARS AGO:
The *Hippocratic Corpus*

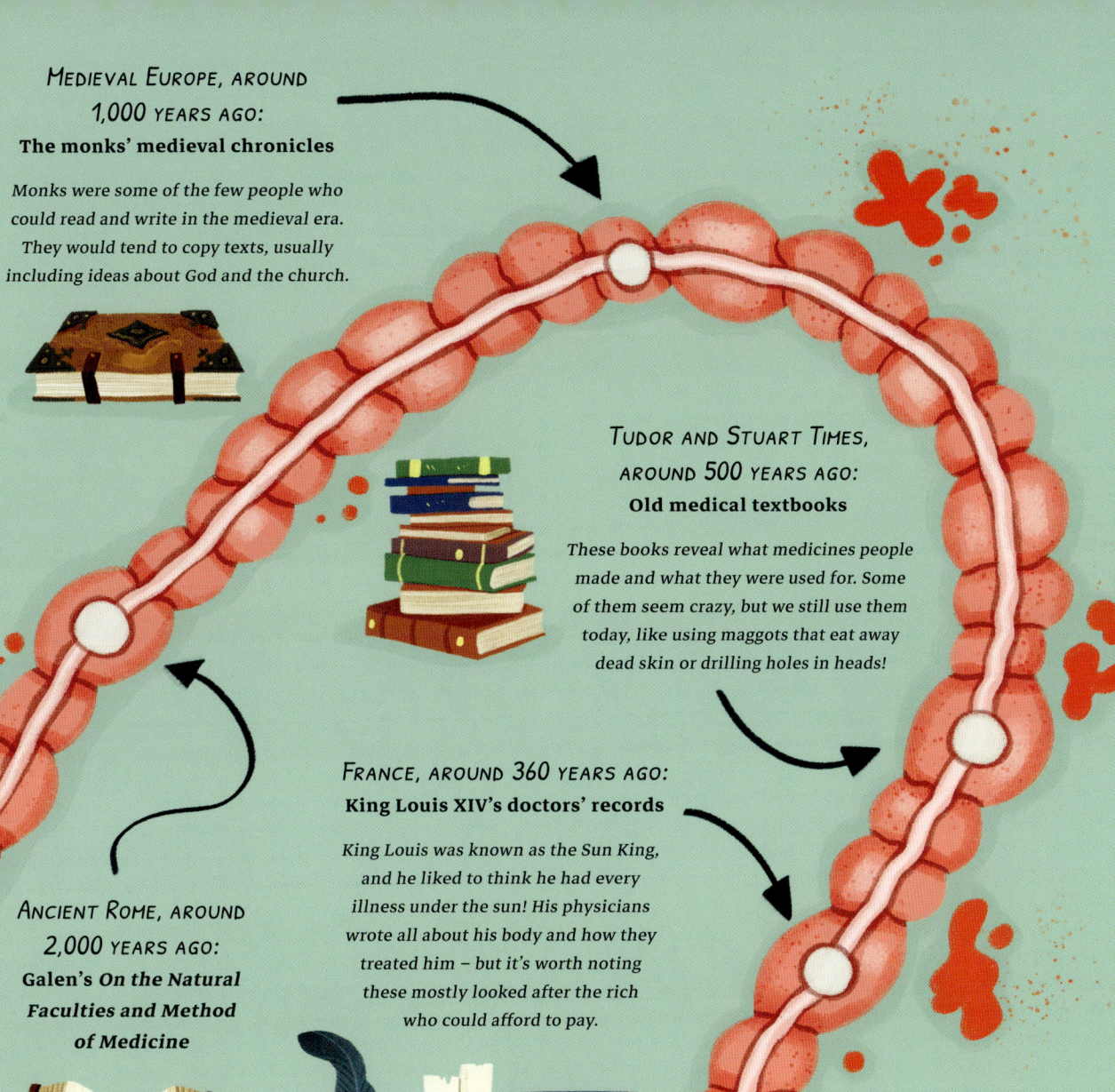

MEDIEVAL EUROPE, AROUND 1,000 YEARS AGO:
The monks' medieval chronicles

Monks were some of the few people who could read and write in the medieval era. They would tend to copy texts, usually including ideas about God and the church.

TUDOR AND STUART TIMES, AROUND 500 YEARS AGO:
Old medical textbooks

These books reveal what medicines people made and what they were used for. Some of them seem crazy, but we still use them today, like using maggots that eat away dead skin or drilling holes in heads!

FRANCE, AROUND 360 YEARS AGO:
King Louis XIV's doctors' records

King Louis was known as the Sun King, and he liked to think he had every illness under the sun! His physicians wrote all about his body and how they treated him – but it's worth noting these mostly looked after the rich who could afford to pay.

ANCIENT ROME, AROUND 2,000 YEARS AGO:
Galen's *On the Natural Faculties and Method of Medicine*

So, what happened to the poor? Well, have you ever heard of old wives' tales? Sometimes Granny knew things that she was told by her granny, who had been told by told by her granny, and so on. Not everything was made into a book, but was just known or believed and passed on through generations. Some of the best recipes and ideas come from a long line of grannies. So, what did the grannies of ancient history pass on to the next generations?

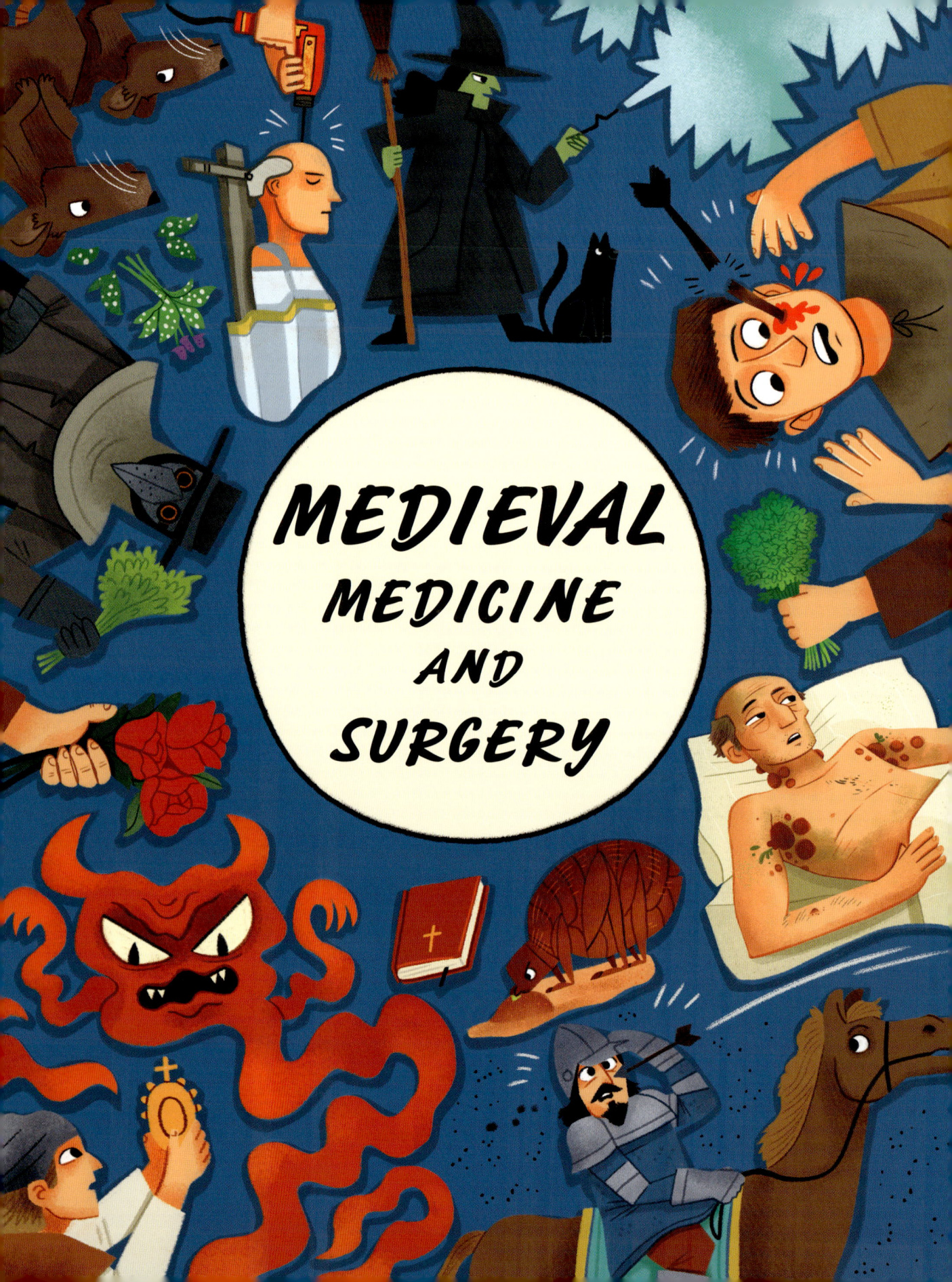

MEDIEVAL
MEDICINE
AND
SURGERY

The medieval era, sometimes called the Dark Ages because scholars thought not much was happening then, stretched from the years 1000 to 1485. It was a time when only the monks and the rich were educated, so they would tell people what to do.

There was lots of fighting in medieval times, so soldiers often suffered terrible wounds from arrows and swords. This meant that surgeons were learning about fixing broken bones, sewing wounds, stopping bleeding and even drilling holes in heads! Get your sharpest knife and most jagged saw at the ready, we're going to do a fast medieval amputation!

It wasn't just about surgical techniques. Doctors would ask God to help with prayers, say chants and incantations and even look to the stars to see what treatments they should use. And what a list of treatments to choose from – herbs and plants grown by monks, and even a headache cure made from garlic – stinky!

Sadly, not all the medicines and surgeries helped. Infections were a big problem, and so many children did not even survive to be ten years old. But lots of people did survive into adulthood, and they had children of their own, luckily for us!

Even more luckily for us, they wrote all about it, so we can learn how our ancestors coped with it all.

Medieval Cures: Herbs and Prayers

When it came to healing ailments, monks would grow plants in special herb gardens. Some were known as **herbalists,** and they would grow, cut and dry herbs and make them into lotions and potions for all sorts of complaints.

WE ALL GET HEADACHES. THEY CAN BE WHAT HAPPENS ON A BAD DAY, OR THEY CAN BE SOMETHING HAPPENING IN THE BRAIN. HEADACHES WERE TREATED WITH HERBS AND PLANTS THAT SMELL SWEET, LIKE ROSES, LAVENDER AND SAGE. SMELLING SOMETHING NICE DOES MAKE US FEEL A BIT BETTER.

FOR FEVERS (HIGH TEMPERATURES), THE MONKS USED A SMELLY HERB CALLED CORIANDER. WE USE CORIANDER NOWADAYS, BUT MORE OFTEN AS GARNISH ON A CURRY!

WOUNDS WERE CLEANED WITH VINEGAR. THAT WOULD HAVE STUNG, BUT IT MIGHT HAVE WORKED BECAUSE THE ACID IN THE VINEGAR WOULD KILL GERMS, ALTHOUGH PEOPLE DIDN'T KNOW ABOUT GERMS YET.

CORIANDER

MINT

HENBANE

SAGE

PLANTS LIKE HENBANE AND HEMLOCK WERE RUBBED ONTO ACHING JOINTS. WHETHER THE HERBS WORKED OR NOT ISN'T KNOWN, BUT RUBBING A SORE JOINT DOES SOMETIMES MAKE IT FEEL BETTER.

FOR UPSET TUMMIES, MEDIEVAL PEOPLE WOULD CHEW OR DRINK ANOTHER SMELLY HERB CALLED MINT. WE STILL USE MINT TODAY. SOMETIMES IT CAN HELP IF WE ARE BLOATED UP WITH GAS.

If herbs seem to have worked, it was thought that it must have been because they influenced the humours, and it was decided that God must have made them for that purpose.

Some herbalists thought that if a plant looked like a body part, then it must have been made by God to cure illnesses of that body part. A plant called spotted lungwort looks a bit like the lungs of someone with tuberculosis, so it was used to treat lung diseases. It was a clever idea, but it didn't work.

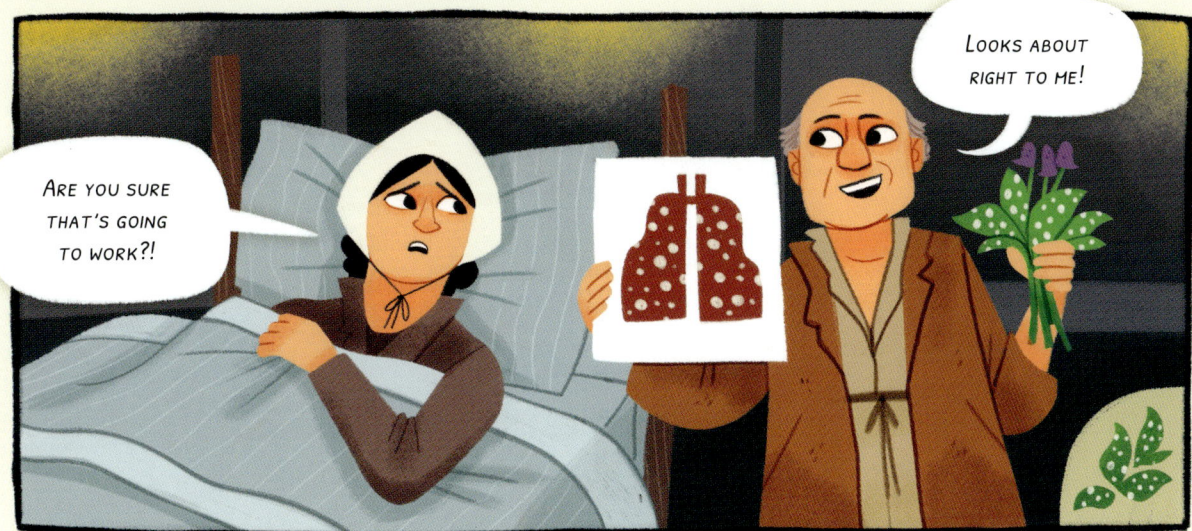

ARE YOU SURE THAT'S GOING TO WORK?!

LOOKS ABOUT RIGHT TO ME!

Not all cures were found in the monastery herb gardens. Sick people could pay monks to pray for them in the monasteries.

There were magical remedies used too – charms said to hold prayers were carried about to ward off evil spirits or to cure illnesses.

One disease called scrofula was thought to be cured by the touch of the King.

Got a bit of a headache after reading all this? Turn the page to find the medieval cure . . .

Ye Olde Braine Hurt Removal Remedy

TAKE EQUAL AMOUNTS OF:

BISHOPWORT (A TYPE OF MINT)

GARLIC

WORMWOOD (A HERB WE USE IN ABSINTHE AND VERMOUTH)

RADISH

HELENIUM (ALSO KNOWN AS SNEEZEWEED!)

CROPLEEK (LEEKS AS WE KNOW THEM!)

HOLLOWLEEK (HAVE YOU EVEN HEARD OF ANY OF THEM?)

METHOD:

- Grab a bowl, any bowl will do, unless it already has something in it!

- Pound the ingredients up together and boil them in a pan of melted butter – make sure to ask your grown-up for help. (At least we've heard of butter, but bishopwart and helenium? Nope, never head of them!)

- Maybe your grown-up has a herb garden just like they had in the monasteries. You might have to ask your gran if you can look through her kitchen cupboards. Just make sure you check the use-by dates!

- Now the mixture is all boiled together and looking yum, you need to keep the mixture in a brass pot until it turns dark red.

- Strain it through a clean cloth, and then smear it on the forehead.

- Oh, you wanted to eat it? Well that's no surprise, it sounds yummy!

- That's sure to help! You'll be back to school in no time.

> IT'S A SHAME YOU CAN'T SMELL IT FROM THERE, BUT I CAN TELL YOU THE AROMAS ARE AMAZING.

For hundreds of years, not many changes happened in medicine. The Church had a big say in matters. Not an actual church, buildings can't speak, but the people who ran the churches had a lot to say.

I HAVE A LOT TO SAY!

Monks would look after the sick, providing care and medicines that they would grow in the monastery herb gardens. Monks were also the people writing and rewriting medical books. They were often much happier to pass on ideas that included God or their own theories, and so religious ideas and prayers played a huge role in ideas about medicine.

They didn't just copy words; they were skilled at drawing and would decorate words in books called illuminated manuscripts. They would add illustrations to make the texts fun, just like we've done here!

In **monasteries,** monks would learn and teach others, passing on what they knew. Only those who could read and write would be able to question them, but they were fellow religious monks, so no questioning took place. But without the monks painstakingly copying and decorating texts, we wouldn't know as much as we know about the Middle Ages.

I HAVE A QUESTION . . . OH WAIT, I'VE CHANGED MY MIND.

Meanwhile, Islamic doctors from Persia (modern-day Iran) and Iraq were making significant changes because they were not stopped from doing so by their church. They had some different ideas. While few medieval texts mentioned children, Ibn Sina (sometimes called Avicenna) wrote about infant care. Sick children should not be bled, he wrote, but a nearby nurse might be bled on their behalf!

EXCUSE ME . . . WHAT!?

Islamic doctors were encouraged to look for new ways to help the sick. They had hospitals called **bimaristans,** and they didn't just look after the rich but also offered help to the poor and to help travellers. Rhazes, a Persian doctor, studied the differences between diseases like measles and smallpox. His works were translated into Latin in 1280.

During the European Renaissance, a time of discoveries and new ideas, Islamic medical texts played a crucial role. The text of Islamic doctors like Rhazes and Ibn Sina (called the *Canon of Medicine*) was translated into Hebrew and Latin, and soon Catholic doctors were able to see their new ideas. These ideas were about surgery but also about medicines and how they might work. When some Christian doctors went on the Crusades, they would see different practices too and bring the new ideas back to Europe with them.

So even if not much happened in medicine for a while, lots of religious trips led to vital ideas sharing.

Surgery

Sometimes, ailments and medical problems needed more than herbs, lotions or potions. They needed surgery, where someone with a strong stomach would use knives and saws to help cure the sick.

Trepanning – A Hole in the Head!

Trepanning is a type of surgery that humans have been performing for over a thousand years. Doctors would use tools of stone and iron to drill a hole into a skull. Not all the way into the brain – that would be a bad idea – but just enough through the skull bone to see the brain underneath and to let evil spirits go free. It is a tricky thing to do, to drill through the skull and not squish into the soft jellylike brain underneath. Well done to them.

It may sound like a crazy idea, but we still drill small holes into the skulls of people who are sick today if their brains are swelling from injury or sickness. This is not done to let out evil spirits, though, it's to lower the pressure. When a brain swells inside the skull, there is nowhere for it to go unless it squeezes out through the hole at the base, which is dangerous enough to kill you. Believe it or not, making a hole in the head can sometimes be a good idea.

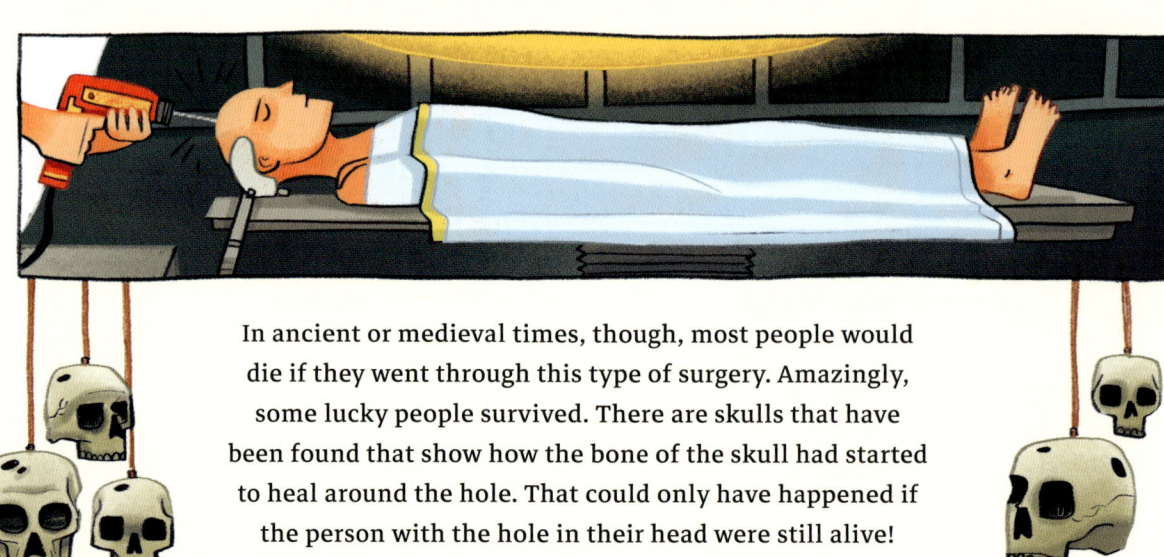

In ancient or medieval times, though, most people would die if they went through this type of surgery. Amazingly, some lucky people survived. There are skulls that have been found that show how the bone of the skull had started to heal around the hole. That could only have happened if the person with the hole in their head were still alive!

Cauterisation - Heat to Stop Bleeding!

What if an injury to the body just wouldn't stop bleeding? Losing too much blood is dangerous.

Blood is needed to carry oxygen from the lungs to the organs, and to carry the waste products away too.

Cells that work to fight off infections are carried in the blood. This is vital to keep us well and alive.

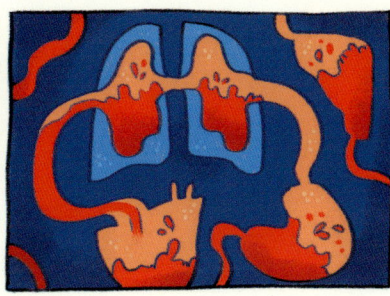
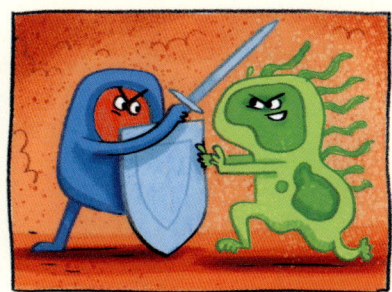

Luckily, ancient and medieval surgeons had ways of dealing with bleeding. Some big blood vessels like arteries or big veins could be stitched with a piece of thread wrapped around them and pulled tight.

But smaller veins can bleed and ooze a lot. Enter cauterisation . . . A rod of iron would be placed in a fire until it was red hot and then it was pressed against the tissue. This would then sizzle and burn and seal the blood inside. That sounds VERY painful, but it was good if it stopped the bleeding.

It's another surgical technique we still use today in operating theatres, but we use smaller tools and a little electricity rather than red hot irons from the fire. Small bleeding blood vessels still sizzle as they are sealed up using heat. Today we use painkillers or anaesthetic medications that mean we can't feel anything if we need to use cauterisation, which is a lot nicer, isn't it? We are lucky indeed, but maybe it's best not to bleed in the first place!

QUICK! We need to amputate a broken leg.

We need to work super fast because the patient is wide awake. Anaesthetics haven't been invented yet.

Firstly, we need someone big and strong to hold the patient down because they'll be able to feel everything.

Let me pick a good spot above where the break (or gangrene) is . . .

If you broke a leg today or made a horrible mess of a limb, the bone doctors could make it right by operating. They can use metal rods and plates and screws to put you back together and help your amazing body heal the bones. The bones might not be exactly the same as they were before the accident, but they'd be OK.

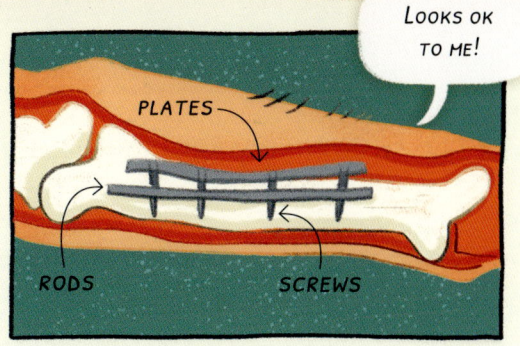

LOOKS OK TO ME!

PLATES

RODS

SCREWS

But back in the Middle Ages, the only way to deal with a nasty fracture was to chop it right off! We call that **amputation**. Sometimes it would be needed if there was a horrible infection or gangrene in the limb that might spread up the body and kill them. Cutting off a limb was a last resort because it was painful, messy and dangerous . . .

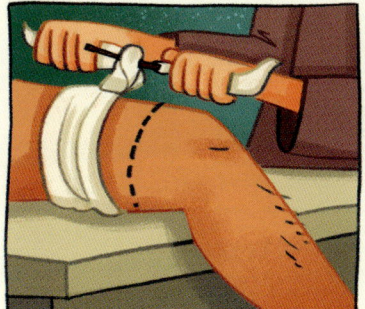

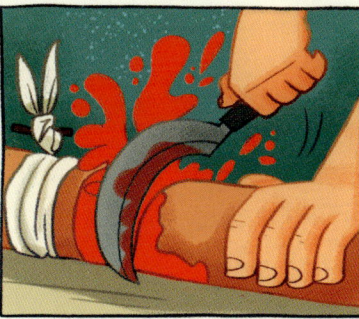

Before cutting anything, doctors would prevent bleeding by putting a tight band called a **tourniquet** above where they were to cut. They would tighten it, so all the blood couldn't drain out.

Then the sharp knives would come out. Sometimes curved knives helped too. Next they would have to cut through the skin and the muscles to the bone.

Bones don't cut easily. You need a saw for that. The bones would crack and break with the saw going back and forth until the limb was eventually free and fell to the floor with a SPLAT!

Where the cut was made, the blood vessels would need to be stopped from bleeding because you can't leave a tourniquet on forever. Doctors would catch hold of the ends and tie a knot around them, but sometimes they would dip the wound in hot tar to seal everything up. Yuck – and OUCH!

Thankfully, not all bone breaks needed an amputation (see page 58). As for the limb that was cut off, you can throw it away because it's no use to anyone anymore. Now which bin should we put it in, refuse or recycling?

The Black Death

In 1348, something scary ravaged Europe, killing one in every three people! Parents, kids, grandparents – everyone was affected. It was a nasty disease called the Black Death.

FLEAS

RATS

DUVET DAY!

Victims wouldn't even have felt it at first when they were bitten by a **flea** – the nibble on the skin would have been so small, but deadly. The fleas were hitching a ride on the fur of black rats that were making their way between countries on ships carrying goods. When the ships arrived at a new port, the rats would jump off to go looking to try the local food, and they would take the fleas along with them. However, fleas don't eat what rats eat – they suck blood from other animals and people, and when they do, they pass the bacteria about.

Victims wouldn't have known that the little flea was spitting the bacteria that causes the dreaded plague into their blood. They would have felt tired, with an achy head. They would have been sick and not wanted to eat anything. It was a day to stay in bed.

But then the **buboes** would have appeared, signalling that they had caught plague. Buboes were swellings of the body parts called lymph nodes that are in the armpits and in the groin between the legs. If you stick your fingers into your armpit (go on!), you can't normally feel the lymph nodes, but you can when you get sick and they can swell up with sticky pus. Plague victims' buboes would have been hard and red and painful, and sometimes buboes even burst open, letting all the stinky pus spew out. Ew.

There were two types of plague during the Black Death: bubonic plague (with the big swollen lymph nodes) and pneumonic (lung) plague, which was the disease in the lungs that was spread by coughs and sneezes. If you caught lung plague, you were going to die pretty fast.

When the plague was finally gone, there were a lot of changes in society. One was that so many people were dead, leaving fewer workers, and so those who survived could ask for more money and to be treated better. At least there was a positive outcome to such a grisly pandemic!

A MYSTERIOUS CLOAKED FIGURE KNOCKS ON AN OLD WOODEN DOOR WITH A CANE . . .

KNOCK KNOCK!

Who's there?

The doctor.

Doctor who?

. . . the plague doctor.

HE LOOKS AT THE PATIENT'S ARMPITS. THEY HAVE RED, SWOLLEN BUBOES. THE DOCTOR POKES THE BUBOES WITH HIS FINGER.

There's not much more I can do.

THE DOCTOR LEAVES THE HOUSE AND PAINTS A RED CROSS ON THE DOOR TO WARN OTHERS THERE IS PLAGUE HERE.

NOBODY KNEW WHAT CAUSED THE PLAGUE. LOTS OF DIFFERENT THINGS WERE BLAMED.

ONE OF THEM WAS MIASMA, WHICH IS BAD AIR. ANY STENCH GOING ABOUT COULD BE SPREADING THE DISEASE.

DOCTOR ALSO BLAMED AN IMBALANCE OF THE FOUR HUMOURS — THOSE PESKY BODY LIQUIDS AGAIN!

OTHERS THOUGHT IT WAS SPELLS CAST BY TROUBLEMAKING WITCHES.

THAT'S WHY DOCTORS WORE THOSE MASKS THAT LOOK LIKE BIRD BEAKS. THEY WOULD PUT HERBS AND FLOWERS — ANYTHING THAT SMELLED NICE — IN THE HOLLOW END, TO WARD OFF THE STINKY MIASMA.

SOME THOUGHT IT WAS A PUNISHMENT SENT BY GOD. GOD MUST HAVE BEEN VERY ANGRY.

ESPECIALLY SEEING AS ANYONE COULD CATCH THE PLAGUE . . .

Uh-oh . . .

A Hole in the Face - Henry V

In 1403, there was a big battle in Shrewsbury, in England. The king, Henry IV, was defending his crown. Henry's son, who was also called Henry, was only 16 years old but he was in the middle of the battle. The king's opponent, Henry Percy from the North of England *(is everyone called Henry?),* lifted the visor on his helmet and was killed by an arrow to the face.

Then the prince was hit in the face by an arrow too! He must have looked up at the wrong moment. The arrow hit him in the cheek just below his eye and got stuck there. Nobody could pull it out as the wooden shaft of the arrow was broken off, leaving the metal tip stuck in his face. It had to be removed before the wound became infected.

A man called John Bradmore was called upon. He was in prison, accused of counterfeiting coins with his metalwork skills, but he was skilled enough to be let out so he could help the prince. He examined the wound, but he couldn't pull the metal point out. He needed to make a special tool that would open the wound and allow him to grab the arrowhead. Thankfully, he managed to get it out.

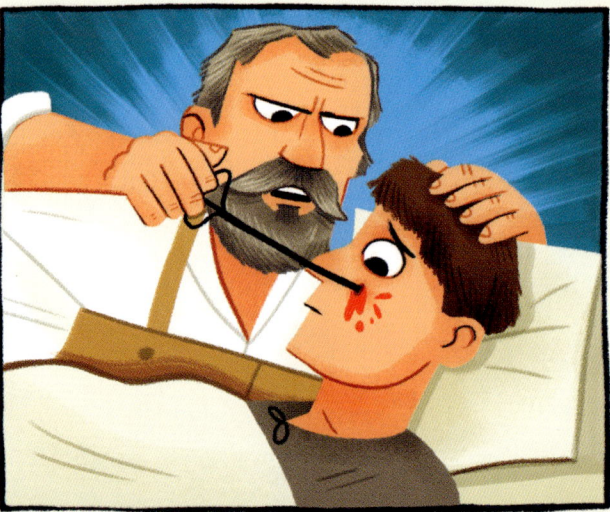

He wasn't finished there. He soaked the hole in Henry's face with wine and honey and changed the dressing regularly to keep it clean.

The alcohol in wine can fight off bacteria and prevent infections, and we still use honey today on wounds that need extra help to heal. Honeybees are very clever!

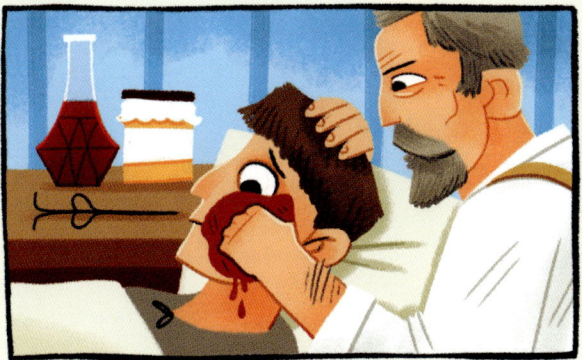

Honey is thought to help wounds because all the sugar in the honey pulls the water out. Bugs and germs need water to live, so if you take their water away, they can't survive in the wounds. It's not just about stopping infections. You know when you hurt yourself, like when you fall and scrape your knees, and the area can go red and be sore, swollen and hot? These are all the signs of **inflammation**. The body is trying to heal itself, but sometimes it needs help. Honey is full of chemicals in it that can help with this too.

TASTES GOOD TOO!

The prince survived, and although he was left with a scar on his cheek, he was OK. One day, he became king himself, and he went on to win a lot of battles. William Shakespeare even wrote a play about him. Whenever you see a portrait of King Henry V, you can tell it is him because he was painted side-on, so the scar on his face wasn't shown. Hooray for John Bradmore's surgical device, and hooray for the healing powers of honey.

So we've had a hole in the head, sawing through bones and a deadly pandemic – what comes next?!

MODERN
MEDICINE

The fifteenth century brought along BIG changes across the world. At the Battle of Bosworth in England, Henry Tudor defeated King Richard III and took his place on the throne, beginning the Tudor dynasty and the start of the English modern era. Meanwhile, the Renaissance in Italy marked the new era in Europe. The invention of the printing press and movable type was spreading ideas fast, and the fall of the city of Constantinople to the Ottomans (from Turkey) marked the end of the Roman Empire.

Sure, the fifteenth century was a long time ago, and Tudor England with Elizabeth I and her rotting teeth doesn't sound very modern. But a lot of modern innovations happened in Europe in the last few hundred years compared to ancient societies and the medieval world (though we have shown they were not as primitive as we sometimes think!).

Some diseases, like sweating sickness in England and the dancing plague in France, have come and gone without us knowing what they even were, but we've got to grips with lots of other diseases and treatments.

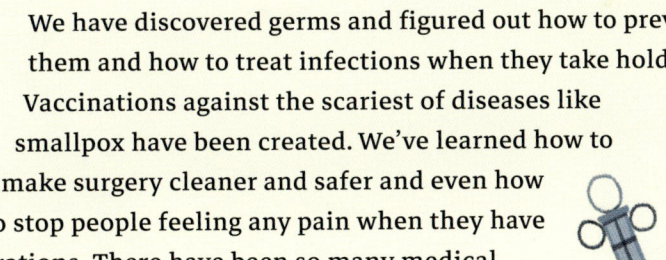

We have discovered germs and figured out how to prevent them and how to treat infections when they take hold. Vaccinations against the scariest of diseases like smallpox have been created. We've learned how to make surgery cleaner and safer and even how to stop people feeling any pain when they have operations. There have been so many medical firsts – even if they were not always accepted in the beginning!

Let's take a look at just how much things have changed in medicine since the fifteenth century.

A Medical Mystery: The Dreaded Sweating Sickness

In 1485, a mysterious disease called the sweating sickness swept through the country. The illness struck down its victims fast. You could be well while eating breakfast and be dead by dinner time. No time for school!

IT STARTED WITH A HORRIBLE FEELING OF DOOM . . .

FOLLOWED BY FEELING SICK WITH ACHES IN THE JOINTS AND A SORE HEAD . . .

AND THEN THE SWEATING STARTED.

Imagine sweating so much that your clothes and your bedsheets were soaked through. You would stink too!

Nobody knew what caused sweating sickness, and we still don't know today. But don't worry – sweating sickness disappeared after a few short outbreaks. It did kill a lot of people though, and some scholars think that it even killed Henry VII's eldest son, Prince Arthur, who likely died of the sweating sickness in 1502. He was only a teenager, but strangely this was a disease that was worse for the middle-aged group of people; it didn't affect the very old and very young. It also affected the wealthy rather than the poor, which is unusual because it is often the crowded houses and dirty water the poor had to use that spread diseases.

It is hard to be sure about a sickness that happened 500 years ago, but we can make guesses based on the evidence we have. Some say it was a germ called hantavirus, which is spread about by rats. Those pesky rats again!

Others think it might have been a toxin, a little chemical that is bad for the body that comes from a bacteria or something mouldy.

Sweating sickness disappeared. The last recorded outbreak was in 1551. To this day, no one knows why. Are you feeling all sweaty now? Don't worry, it won't be sweating sickness, but you might just want a bath!

Smallpox, Scars and Vaccines

Smallpox was a very contagious disease that killed one in three people who caught it. Anyone who had the disease would have felt sick, had achy joints and a painfully sore head.

They would also have found lumps on their skin called pustules that were red, hot, itchy and full of pus.

Pus is made when the body fights germs with white blood cells.

They break down the germs and what's left is a gooey, stinky mixture that we can squeeze out of abscesses and boils.

Thankfully, since then, a vaccine has been made that stops us getting the disease. In fact, the disease has been irradicated (it no longer exists in humans). It has been nearly fifty years since the last case of smallpox happened, in 1977. We don't even need to use the vaccines any more.

VACCINES MAKE A HUGE DIFFERENCE TO THE HEALTH AND WELL-BEING OF EVERYBODY. THEY PREVENT SICKNESS BY GIVING THE BODY A TINY DOSE OF THE DISEASE.

THOSE CLEVER WHITE BLOOD CELLS IN THE BODY THAT FIGHT OFF DISEASES CAN THEN LEARN ABOUT THE NEW GERM AND CAN MAKE ANTIBODIES THAT FIGHT THE DISEASE IF IT COMES BACK.

BUT HOW DID WE LEARN ABOUT VACCINES? IT WAS A CLEVER EXPERIMENT . . .

Edward Jenner was an English doctor, who in 1796 used another virus called cowpox to vaccinate a young boy, eight-year-old James Phipps. Why cowpox? Well, he had noticed that the milkmaids who tended the cows sometimes contracted the disease cowpox, and if they did, they were unlikely to ever get smallpox. He thought that the diseases must have been similar, and so catching the milder disease of cowpox might be worth doing, to prevent the worse disease of smallpox.

James Phipps became immune to smallpox. When he was exposed to it, he didn't get sick. He was lucky it worked – he could have died! I wouldn't have wanted to be the first to be experimented on, would you? Luckily, today we have strict rules about medical experiments.

While Edward Jenner gets the modern-day credit for first coming up with vaccines in the West, elsewhere in the world there has been the use of variolation (another name for vaccinations or jabs) for centuries. In the Ottoman Empire and in ancient China, it was known that taking a tiny amount of pus from a smallpox sufferer and pushing it into a little cut in the skin could prevent infections.

Hooray for vaccines and the eradication of smallpox! But there were more diseases that were a complete mystery. Ready to come dancing?

IN THE SUMMER OF **1518** IN STRASBOURG, FRANCE, A WOMAN CALLED FRAU TROFFEA STEPS OUT OF HER HOUSE.

Good morning, Frau Troffea!

Good morning! Let's dance!

SHE STARTS DANCING IN THE STREET. SHE JIGS AND JIVES AND WON'T STOP.

Great dancing Frau Troffea! Can anyone join in?

A CROWD GATHERS TO WATCH, AND PEOPLE CLAP AND ENCOURAGE HER, CHEERING HER ON.

The more the merrier!

MORE PEOPLE JOIN IN. FOUR HUNDRED PEOPLE DANCE IN THE STREET. SOME DANCE SO MUCH, THEY COLLAPSE AND DIE OF EXHAUSTION.

The Heart Is a Pump?

In the seventeenth century, a young man called Hugh Montgomery was climbing up a tree one day, and when he put out his foot to rest it on a branch – CRACK! – it broke beneath his weight. He fell and landed so badly that a branch went through his skin and ribs. OUCH.

He was lucky that he survived, and the broken branch did not go right through his heart! Instead, the branch just made a big hole. He didn't get an infection, but the hole made by the branches didn't heal over. He was left for the rest of his life with a hole in his chest. Anyone who got close enough could see Hugh's heart beating!

Hugh's accident gained the attention of Doctor William Harvey. When Doctor Harvey met Hugh and saw his heart through the hole in his chest wall, he thought it was so amazing that he took him to see King Charles I of England.

The King was amazed too, and he even put his finger in the hole and touched Hugh's heart! Would you have put your finger in the hole to touch Hugh Montgomery's heart? I would have!

Doctor Harvey became well known for his work in understanding our hearts. He learned that veins in the body contained little bits of tissue in them called valves.

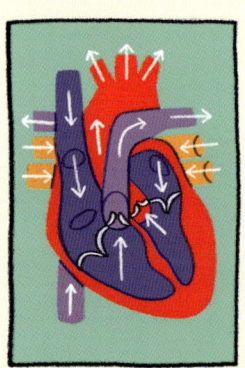

All the valves, wherever they are in the body, point towards the heart and stop blood from flowing away from the heart. He told us how the heart pushed blood around the body, and it came back to the heart to be sent off again.

Before that, it was thought that blood was made from the food we eat, went round the body once and was used up by the body all in one go. Now with William Harvey's work, we could see that the body pushed the same blood round and round. It was a new way of thinking about the heart.

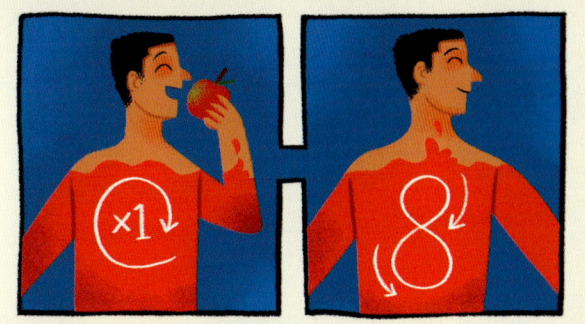

In the 1500s, a Spanish physician called Servetus, and even earlier in the 1200s, a Muslim physician called Ibn-al Nafis, both described two separate types of blood systems. Bright **red** blood and **purple** blood were seen as different things. Later it was understood that blood is red when full of oxygen and darker when the oxygen is used up.

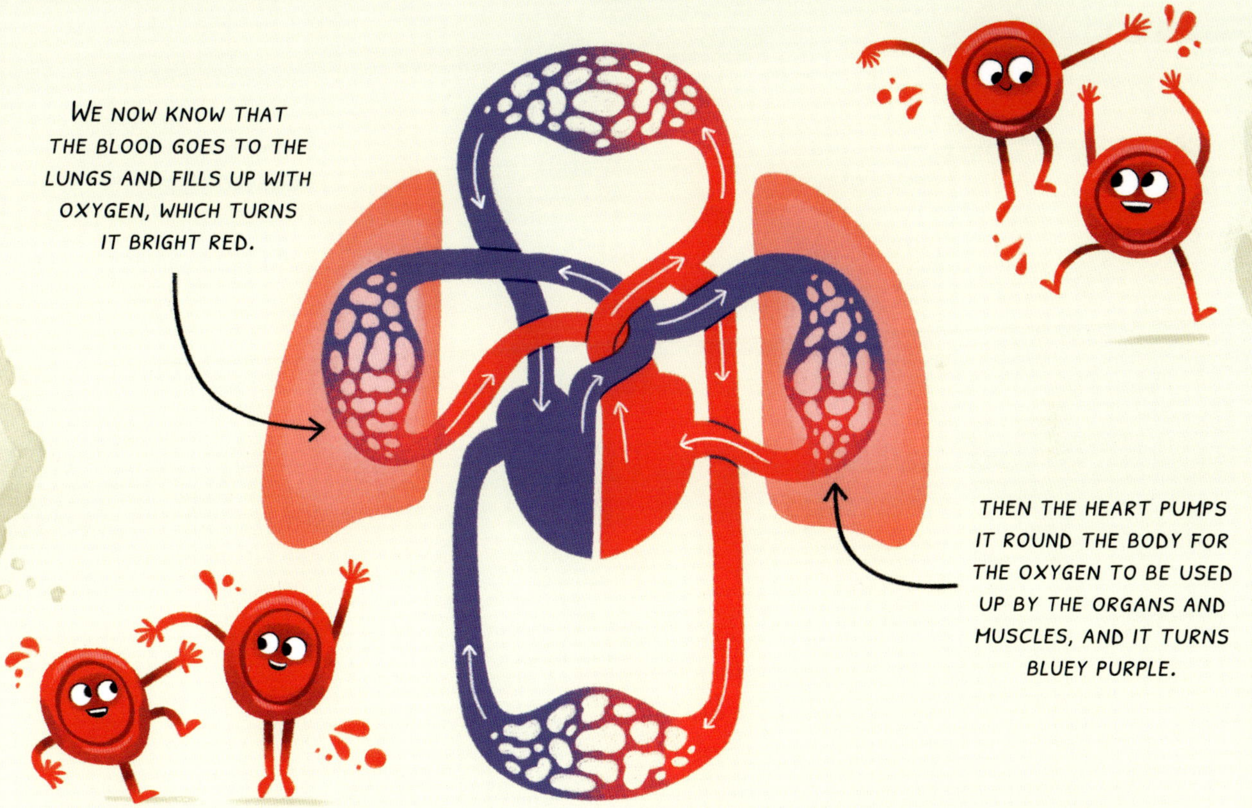

WE NOW KNOW THAT THE BLOOD GOES TO THE LUNGS AND FILLS UP WITH OXYGEN, WHICH TURNS IT BRIGHT RED.

THEN THE HEART PUMPS IT ROUND THE BODY FOR THE OXYGEN TO BE USED UP BY THE ORGANS AND MUSCLES, AND IT TURNS BLUEY PURPLE.

Not everyone agreed with William Harvey at first. It is always hard for new ideas to catch on, especially when they question what people have been thinking and teaching for hundreds of years.

Doctors learned more about how bodies worked by dissecting (cutting up) dead ones. And you won't believe how they got hold of the dead bodies . . .

We're Going Bodysnatching

Doctors and surgeons need to know as much as they can about our bodies. What are all the bits, and how do they fit together? How do our bodies work, and how do they go wrong? The best way to answer those questions is to go and have a look at the body – not just the outside, but the inside too.

Doctors had to cut bodies open. The best bodies to use are dead ones – they don't mind as much! Sometimes they could get dead bodies, called **cadavers**, from the gallows, where criminals had been hanged for their crimes.

I DIDN'T THINK I'D BE SELLING BODIES WHEN I GREW UP!

There was a problem, though. There were a lot more doctors and medical students needing dead bodies to dissect than there were dead bodies available. The only way they could get their hands (and knives) on dead bodies was to **steal** them.

Once the dead had been buried, the doctors would go out in the dark of night. They needed special wooden shovels so they would make less noise. It was risky – if they were caught, they could be in trouble. While it wasn't illegal to steal a dead body (they were thought to be no one's property and therefore could not technically be stolen), if they stole any of the clothing that the dead body had been buried in, they could be arrested for grave robbing! Isn't that silly? Sure, go ahead, take the body, but make sure you leave behind the nightdress they were buried in!

When the doctors and medical students decided it was too risky, they paid other people to do it for them. They were called the **resurrectionists** – but nobody liked them stealing bodies very much.

I DON'T LOVE IT EITHER!

People came up with ingenious ways to try and stop the bodysnatchers. They made iron cages called **mortsafes** that were placed over the graves and far too heavy for the resurrectionists to move. There are many still lying around in graveyards today.

Watchtowers were built in graveyards so that relatives could stay and keep a lookout over the grave both day and night. How long for? Well, for as long as it takes a dead body to go all mouldy and not be of use to the surgeons.

That might take a few weeks. Relatives that stayed by the gravesides would have a warm fire in the watchtower and a roof over their heads.

When anything stirred in the graveyard after dark, they would chase them away or fire guns into the dark to warn them off. Bad news for the doctors who needed bodies, but good for the relatives of the dead.

Antiseptics

Two huge discoveries were made in medical treatments in the modern era: **antiseptics**, which prevent infection, and **anaesthetics**, which reduce pain.

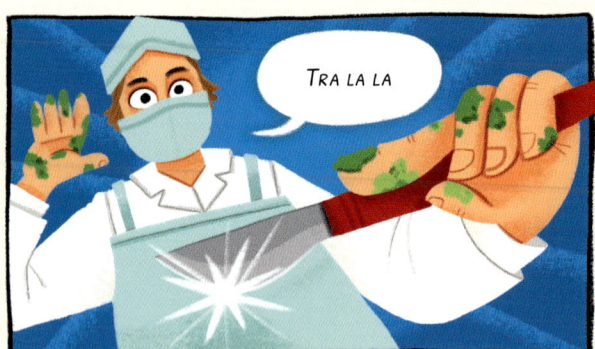

When surgeons cut into bodies, there was a chance that the germs on their knives and their hands would get into their patients. Annoyingly, germs are so small, we can't see them with our eyes alone. Because surgeons couldn't see the germs, they did not wash their hands or their instruments, or the operating tables or even the aprons that they wore.

When microscopes were invented around the 1600s, we could see the germs, but we had to figure out how to stop them causing diseases. Enter Joseph Lister, a surgeon from Scotland who figured out that he could spray wounds and the air around operations with carbolic acid to possibly prevent infections.

In 1871, Queen Victoria felt she had a sore armpit. She scratched at it, and it turned into a great big abscess – that's like a great big spot – the size of an orange!

She called on Dr Lister, and he went to her castle with his carbolic spray machine and a sharp knife. He sprayed around her armpit, then he cut open the abscess and drained out all the pus.

The queen survived and she didn't get an infection. Hooray for Lister and his carbolic spray!

Now we regularly use antiseptics by cleaning the skin before we do any operations. We clean the bedsheets too, plus the operating instruments and the beds. And very importantly, we thoroughly clean our hands.

Anaesthetics

Imagine having an operation without anaesthetics . . .

BEFORE THE 1840s, SURGEONS HAD TO WORK VERY FAST BECAUSE ANYBODY HAVING AN OPERATION WOULD HAVE BEEN WIDE AWAKE AND HAVE FELT EVERYTHING!

IT WAS ALSO VERY TRICKY TO OPERATE ON SOMEONE WHO WAS WRIGGLING AND FIGHTING BACK.

IN AMERICA IN 1846, A SUBSTANCE CALLED ETHER WAS USED THAT MADE THE PATIENT GO TO SLEEP AND NOT FEEL ANY OF THE OPERATION. IF ANYONE WERE TO SNIFF THE VAPOURS FROM IT, THEY WOULD NOD OFF.

IT WASN'T IDEAL, THOUGH. IT COULD HURT THE LUNGS WHEN BREATHED IN, AND IT ALSO HAD A HABIT OF CATCHING FIRE AS IT WAS VERY FLAMMABLE.

In 1847, another Scottish doctor called James Young Simpson was experimenting with a substance called chloroform with two of his doctor friends one evening. They each took a sniff from the bottle that was passed around after dinner. It knocked them all out cold! When they woke up, they realised they had found something that could help people sleep during operations. They put it to work at once. But it didn't all go perfectly. One 15-year-old girl called Hannah Greener died when she was given chloroform. She was only having a toenail taken off but had a bad reaction to the anaesthetic!

Another problem was that being able to operate for longer meant that more germs had a chance to get in the body and cause more infections. When we started to use anaesthesia, more people died of infections! They needed those antiseptics too.

When Poo Got Into the Water: Cholera and the Broad Street Pump

When poo gets into water that we drink, we can get very sick.
But that wasn't always understood.

In the last two hundred years, there have been seven pandemics of a terrible disease called cholera. In China in 1817, an outbreak spread to Southeast Asia, Japan and Eastern Siberia, Russia. The disease was carried along routes where people travelled and traded. Wherever people went, cholera followed them.

In the nineteenth century, cholera was on a killing spree all over the world. In Mecca in 1846, more than 15,000 died. Three years later, there was a major outbreak in France. It spread across America too, where the US President James K. Polk died of it with thousands of others.

Another outbreak hit a very busy area of London called Soho, in the 1850s. The sewers were full of poo and bacteria were overflowing into the water that was being used for drinking and washing.

Once inside people's tummies, the water was making them very sick. Cholera bacteria multiplies in people's warm insides, and a nasty toxin (pieces of the bacteria) gives people sickness and diarrhoea.

After a while, all the fluids have come out, leaving victims dehydrated, meaning they've run out of water! We need water inside us to live.

How did they figure out what was causing the outbreak? A very clever doctor called John Snow had a feeling that it was not just bad air making everyone sick. With the help of a local vicar, the Reverend Henry Whitehead, who did not like seeing his congregation so ill, he studied all the cases of cholera in Soho. He made a map of the streets and marked on them where the sick people lived. Something stood out! There were more than 500 cases of cholera in just ten days, and they were all getting their water from the same water pump! That was the connection.

This was a time before indoor plumbing, and many had no taps at kitchen sinks; instead they went out to the pump. They were all drinking the same dirty water.

As there were no toilets and running water, there were no proper sewers, either. Poo and waste were put into cesspits, big holes under the houses. When they were full, night soil men came and emptied them out. Sometimes the sludge spilled over and slipped into the water.

Not many people believed Dr Snow, but he had a solution. He took the handle off the pump so nobody could use it. People stopped getting sick. This was looking after the health of the public in action. New fields of medicine, all about public health (the health of everyone) and epidemiology (studying the statistics and figures of a disease) were born. Four years later in 1858, when even more terrible things happened with sewage that made the River Thames stink terribly, big new sewers and pumping stations were built to help look after everyone's health.

It was such an important moment in the history of medicine that there is a monument on the spot where the Broad Street Pump once stood.

Antibiotics and Alexander Fleming

One day in 1928, a scientist called Alexander Fleming left his laboratory, shut the door and went on holiday. It's not a great start to a medical discovery story, is it? But wait for it . . .

When he came back from his holiday, he found that his petri dishes had gone all mouldy. Ew. Petri dishes are the small round dishes that scientists use to grow and study germs.

He realised that where the mould had been growing, his germs had NOT been growing. It looked like something in the mould was killing the bacteria. He called it penicillin. This was the first antibiotic, a substance that could be used to fight infections. What a discovery! Could this be used to kill the bacteria that were causing deadly infections?

So far, we had antiseptics – substances that could kill germs and **prevent infections from happening**. Remember Queen Victoria's armpit? Now we had substances that could stop infections that had **already started**. We could now cure some bacterial infections!

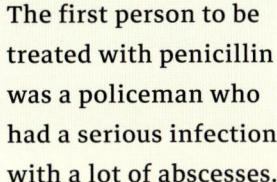

HOORAY!

OH NO!

The first person to be treated with penicillin was a policeman who had a serious infection with a lot of abscesses.

Within a day of treatment with penicillin, he was much better.

This was good news, but sadly they did not have enough of it, and he later died.

Scientists had to figure out how to make much more of it so that people like him could survive.

More scientists in Oxford, England and in the United States joined in with the research until they figured out how to make big batches of the medicine, especially to help people during the Second World War. Medical techniques and surgeries often do better in times of war when governments invest in treatments for wounded troops. Their work made a big impact, straight away. Antibiotics could now be used to stamp out nasty infections.

Doctors Fleming, Chain and Florey won the Nobel Prize for medicine in 1945. The Nobel Prizes are big prestigious awards given each year to exciting discoveries and work in the sciences and the arts. There's even a prize for the person who has contributed to world peace. And did you know that the man who started giving out the Nobel Prizes, Alfred Nobel, was the inventor of dynamite? BANG.

Bone Setting

Have you ever broken a bone? Children's bones can be set in place and heal quicker than adults' bones.

For grown-ups, it can take longer because their bones are a lot harder and less bendy. But even if we can put them back together, breaking a bone is not a good idea!

Breaking bones didn't always need an operation or an amputation. Sometimes they could be manipulated by hand back into place, and the bones would heal themselves in a few weeks or months if they were held in place.

In some places around the world, there were families or individuals who were known as bonesetters. They were skilled at setting and healing broken bones and dislocations (that's when bones in the joints like the shoulders or kneecaps come away from each other and need to be put back). Within communities, everyone knew who to go to if they broke a bone or had a joint problem. Famous bonesetters include . . .

Thomas family

HOME: Wales

....

NOTABLE MEMBERS: Evan, who was adopted when he was washed ashore after a boat wreck; Hugh Owen, who invented the Thomas splint.

....

LEGACY: The Thomas splint is still used today to keep broken bones in place while they heal!

Sally Mapp

NICKNAME: 'Crazy Sally Mapp' – she was quite fierce and shouted a lot!

....

TAUGHT BY: Her father

....

PHYSICALITY: Big and strong, which comes in handy when moving broken bones!

What do you do if you break a bone? You go and see the doctor straight away, and they will do an X-ray to see what's happened. I bet Sally Mapp would have loved to have X-rays, painkillers and anaesthetics too, but they had not been invented yet.

Now Wash Your Hands!

You know how your parents and teachers are always telling you to wash your hands? They say it all the time . . .

after you've been to the toilet,

before you eat your lunch,

and especially after you've picked your nose!

There is a very good reason to wash our hands, but we have not always understood how important it is. In the nineteenth century in Europe, there was one man who figured it out, but nobody believed him!

Ignaz Semmelweis

BORN: 1818 in Budapest, Hungary

DIED: 1865 in Vienna, Austria

JOB: A doctor learning about anatomy by dissecting dead bodies. He also worked in other parts of the hospital where mothers were having children.

Semmelweis noticed that more of the new mums got sick and died when the doctors were attending them, rather than the midwives. What were the doctors doing differently? Perhaps, he thought, the doctors were taking something with them, on their hands, and infecting the mums having babies. What could it be?

He did some experiments, and he found out that by simply washing their hands in between seeing dead bodies and patients, the doctors might not cause so many infections. He couldn't wait to tell the other doctors what he found.

Rather than saying "WELL DONE, GOOD JOB", the other doctors were very angry with him. They did not like being blamed, especially for spreading something that couldn't even be seen. They said . . .

DON'T BE SO SILLY. WE CAN'T POSSIBLY BE MAKING THE MOTHERS SICK. WE ARE CLEVER DOCTORS!

KEEP YOUR DIRTY HANDS OFF MY BABY!

They refused to wash their hands, and Semmelweis was not surprised at all to see that the mothers kept getting sick. But he could not get through to the other doctors. Ignaz Semmelweis wrote letters about it to anyone who might listen to him, but nobody did. He would not let it go.

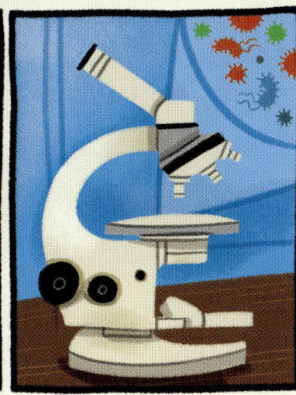

His fellow doctors said he must be mentally ill, and they tricked him into going to an asylum, where he was treated very badly. His own hand was cut, leading to an infection.

Sadly, Ignaz Semmelweis died before others realised he was right. He'd had no proof that germs existed, but later people started to understand that there were indeed tiny particles that could cause diseases that were being spread about on hands.

With the use of microscopes, the tiny particles Semmelweis believed were causing disease could be seen.

Germs can be washed away with soap and water – so remember to always wash your hands!

Index

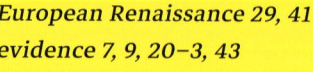

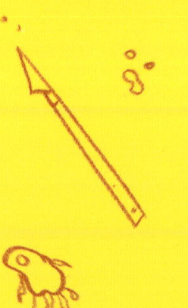
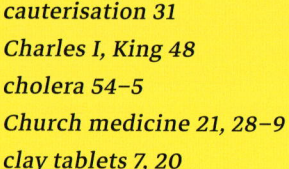

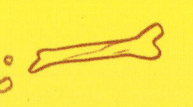

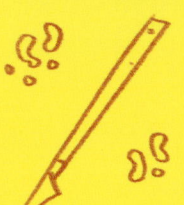